MW01031999

Whispers
from Above

&

Reflections
from the Heart

By Anne Marie McDonnell Vale, Ph. D.

The photograph on the front cover is courtesy of Michael Vale.

Dedication

THIS BOOK IS DEDICATED TO SOME SPECIAL PEOPLE who have encouraged me. First of all, I want to remember my beloved parents, George and Rita McDonnell, who gave me the gift of life and their unconditional love always. I am also very grateful to my husband, Michael, for his constant love and support. Finally, I would like to thank Ronni Miller, Founder of the Write it Out Program and my expressive writing teacher at the Center for Building Hope in Lakewood Ranch, Florida. Her encouragement has been invaluable, and this book would not have been possible without her skillful direction and tutelage.

Author's Background

DR. ANNE MARIE McDONNELL VALE graduated from St. Mary's Academy, Bay View, an independent all-girls Catholic high school in East Providence, Rhode Island. After graduation, she received a special talent piano scholarship to study music at Rhode Island College, where she completed her bachelor's and master's degrees in music education. In 1999, Anne Marie attained her Ph. D. in organizational leadership from Regent University in Virginia Beach, and subsequently taught as an adjunct professor in Regent's graduate leadership studies program.

Anne Marie was a public school elementary music specialist and classroom teacher for twenty-nine years in the North Providence School Department. She received honorable recognition as the "North Providence Teacher of the Year" in 2006. She also served as the music director at St. Casimir's Lithuanian Catholic Church in Providence for over thirty years.

Anne Marie, who lives with her husband, Michael in Sarasota, Florida enjoys playing music at local nursing facilities and in the surrounding community. Anne Marie and Michael are parishioners of the Church of the Incarnation in Sarasota.

If you wish to contact Anne Marie, her e-mail address is amcd@pobox. com. She would love to hear from you.

Acknowledgements

THE WRITINGS IN THIS BOOK REFLECT LESSONS in kindness, forgiveness, and perseverance taught to me by many special people throughout my life: my parents, my Godparents, my husband, my extended family, my teachers at St. Mary's Academy, Bay View, my professors at Rhode Island College and Regent University, my parish family at St. Casimir's Church, clergy members and parishioners at churches I've attended, my comrades in the North Providence School Department, my former students and their families, my close friends and neighbors, my friends in the Waldenstrom's community, and ultimately, the Good Lord Who created me and continues to sustain my life every day.

St. John Paul II reminds each of us:

Have no fear of moving into the unknown. Simply step out fearlessly knowing that I am with you, therefore no harm can befall you; all is very, very well. Do this in complete faith and confidence.

This message is very comforting and inspiring to me. I hope the words and pictures I share in this book will likewise provide comfort and inspiration to all of my readers.

—ANNE MARIE

Table of Contents

PART III
Sensory Perceptions

Introduction

As a loyal Catholic, I pledge my allegiance to the teaching authority of the Church. Pope Francis challenges all members of the Church to transcend the temptation to remain self-referential and to reach out to everyone in our world. This book is an integral aspect of my response to the Holy Father's invitation.

This is a treasured personal collection of poetry, fiction, essays, biographies, and photographs. Each entry is concise and self-contained so you can start and finish reading wherever you wish. The different genres provide the reader with some variety as well.

In April of 2012, I was diagnosed with a rare non-Hodgkin's lymphoma known as Waldenstrom's macroglobulinemia (WM). As of this writing, I am on "watch and wait" and currently do not need treatment since I am generally asymptomatic. My life is beautiful, and I am very blessed. It is filled with the love and compassion of family and friends. Much of my writing is based on my gratitude and admiration for others. I've also learned that having a chronic condition does not define who you are.

The title of this book, *Whispers from Above and Reflections from the Heart*, summarizes my basic philosophy for living a fulfilled and joyous life. I believe that the Holy Spirit whispers into my soul and guides me every moment of my life; hence, the reflections contained in these pages are my personal responses to those whispers. Just as deep waters flow gently under a bridge, serenely touching the horizon, I pray that my words flow gently into your innermost being, serenely touching your soul.

Fifty per cent of the proceeds from the sale of this book will be donated to benefit the International Waldenstrom's Macroglobulinemia Foundation. I am optimistic that ongoing research funded by IWMF will ultimately lead to a cure for WM in the near future.

PART I
Close Family Ties

CHAPTER ONE

Waiting at the Edge of a Rainbow

I WAS SITTING IN THE EXAMINING ROOM, expecting to hear that the results of my bone marrow biopsy were just fine so I could quickly leave and enjoy the rest of the day at the beach. It was April of 2012, and I had just moved to Sarasota, Florida about three years ago. After living in Rhode Island most of my life, I was enjoying the sunshine and all the amenities the Gulf Coast had to offer.

A month earlier, I had a routine blood test that showed an excess amount of an unidentified protein. My family doctor didn't think it was serious, but he suggested that I see a hematologist. It seemed ridiculous to me that I was even seeing a hematologist. Still I followed my doctor's advice and had several blood tests and a urine test. No specific problems were identified. So I was told that a bone marrow biopsy was needed, and I willingly complied. After all, I had a bone marrow biopsy in my twenties, and everything turned out just fine. At the time, I was just a little anemic so I was simply told to take some iron pills. No big deal! This time, though, the situation was different.

My new hematologist cheerfully entered the room after I waited restlessly for about twenty minutes, which seemed like forever. He then promptly announced that I had Waldenstrom's macroglobulinemia (WM)! I thought he was joking, at first. It sounded like one of those concocted terms you hear in a Disney film! But this was no joke.

He then told me, "It's similar to lymphoplasmacytic lymphoma and a sub-type of non-Hodgkin's lymphoma." Still, he was also quick to say, "Don't worry; it's the best kind of cancer to have. It's very slow moving, and it's extremely rare. You're much more apt to die with it than from it. Go home and enjoy the rest of your day. You might never get really sick."

This couldn't possibly be happening to me! There had to be some mistake, especially since I generally felt good. Yes, I had been coping with idiopathic peripheral neuropathy in my feet for twenty years. My feet tingled and my legs and toes sometimes cramped, but I dealt with it stoically. I suddenly felt like I entered another realm, as if I was having a bad dream. Despite being in a daze, I did manage to ask the doctor to write down this ominous-sounding term, *Waldenstrom's macroglobulinemia* (WM), on a piece of paper. I stared at it in disbelief for a few minutes. The doctor then told me to come back in six months for some routine blood work, and that was it! I walked out into the parking lot in a stunned, confused, and depressed state.

Now, my hematologist/oncologist, who has since moved back North, was a super nice guy and a competent physician. However, as he proclaimed my WM diagnosis with an air of optimism, I was feeling a sense of terror. Why? Well, to sum up WM in a few sentences, without giving me at least an elementary understanding of this very rare non-Hodgkin's lymphoma, only caused me to imagine the very worst! I kept thinking to myself, "He must be hiding something from me." However, in retrospect, I don't think that was his intention at all.

Still feeling somewhat frightened and confused, I called my doctor a few days later and asked if I could be sent to another cancer clinic for a second opinion. Fortunately the appointment was promptly and easily arranged just one week later. Only this time, the oncologist I saw told me quite emphatically that I did *not* have WM. Instead he diagnosed me with the very early stages of marginal zone lymphoma (MZL). He once again, like the previous doctor, assured me that it was nothing to be worried about.

However, for the next year, I was required to see both of my oncologists. I would see my local doctor every three months and my other consulting oncologist every six months. This was challenging since each was insisting that his diagnosis was the correct one. I also continued to feel basically fine, other than my chronic peripheral neuropathy, which I had been tolerating for two decades. Both doctors told me that my neuropathy must be due to something else since it's been such a long-term condition. In other words, it's just idiopathic, with evidently no identifiable cause. I'd been told that many times over the past twenty years

For over a year, I did my best to conduct Internet searches on both Waldenstrom's macroglobulinemia and marginal zone lymphoma. Of course, I am not an experienced medical doctor so it was not always easy to discern and comprehend the plethora of information I discovered. I was able to learn that both diseases have overlapping features and therefore it is not always easy to provide an accurate initial diagnosis. OK, now that's great! I might have something very rare, that only about six in one million people are diagnosed with in the United States annually. My original doctor still swears that I have the early stages of Waldenstrom's macroglobulinemia! The consulting doctor continues to tell me I have the early stages of marginal zone lymphoma. They both tell me not to worry! Yikes!

Now, it's May of 2013, and I was *still* not sure if I have WM or not! One day as I was doing an Internet search I came across a web site for the Bing Center for Waldenstrom's Macroglobulinemia at the Dana-Farber Cancer Institute in Boston. I learned that the Bing Center is one of the premier WM research institutes in the world. So I quickly sent an e-mail message with some basic WM questions. Staff members provided more information in a few e-mails than I had garnered in the past year. They were so willing to help me in every way possible. An appointment was easily and promptly scheduled.

So, in June of 2013, my husband and I traveled to Boston. I can't say enough wonderful things about the Bing Center at Dana-Farber! It is internationally renowned for its research, diagnosis, and treatment of Waldenstrom's macroglobulinemia. I met with a knowledgeable doctor whose analysis of my original bone marrow biopsy results and previous blood lab results reaffirmed my initial diagnosis of WM.

Dr. Steven Treon, the Director of the Bing Center for Waldenstrom's Macroglobulinemia, is known worldwide for his expertise as a distinguished WM researcher. His achievements are numerous. Using whole genome sequencing, Dr. Treon and members of his research team have discovered specific genetic mutations that the vast majority of WM patients have. This not only helps to diagnose the condition accurately, but it also assists in the development of targeted therapies in treating the malignancy.

The following summary provides a general description of WM. Our white blood cells (called lymphocytes) come in three different types. The B cells make antibodies to fight infection. WM evidently starts when there is a genetic mutation to a single B white blood cell. Malignant B cells start to multiply uncontrollably. These cells overproduce huge amounts of a protein known as immunoglobin M (commonly called IgM). These malignant cells primarily grow in the bone marrow. This is why a bone marrow biopsy is needed to diagnose WM.

The elevated level of IgM in the blood (the protein that's secreted by the malignant B cells) can crowd out red blood cells, other white blood cells, and plasma, causing a variety of problems. If the IgM level gets very high, there may be a hyperviscosity syndrome, meaning that the blood is so thick that it cannot circulate properly. Symptoms can greatly vary from patient to patient.

At least 25% of WM patients are asymptomatic and do not need treatment. I am blessed to be one of those who are on "watchful waiting." I simply see the doctor every six months for blood tests to check on the level of protein (IgM) in my blood. I may not need treatment for many years or ever at all!

In March of 2015, I made a second trip to Dana-Farber to have another bone marrow biopsy, which still shows only 5 – 10% percent infiltration in the marrow. Also, this time, the bone marrow biopsy included a report that was not available to me the first time. I was tested for a common genetic mutation present in 95% of WM patients. I have the MYD88 genetic mutation, which now unequivocally confirms my initial diagnosis of Waldenstrom's macroglobulinemia.

In the last couple of years, I've researched hours and hours online, attended two conferences, including the national WM conference held annually. I continue to interact with other patients on a Facebook page for Waldenstrom's macroglobulinemia patients and have developed friends while gaining more detailed knowledge along the way.

It is true that some WM patients do indeed suffer from various forms of neuropathy. I happen to be one of them! It is believed that the elevated levels of IgM may adversely affect a certain percentage of patients neurologically.

There is still much more to be learned in terms of the exact nature of how WM correlates to various types of neuropathy. In my case, weekly sessions with Dr. Gaoxiong Zhu, my wonderful acupuncturist, helps tremendously in decreasing the unpleasant symptoms of my small fiber peripheral neuropathy while improving my micro-circulation.

Still, I want to emphasize that I am only sharing my own personal experience with alternative medicine, and I am not making any specific recommendations since I am not qualified to do so. Every case is different and WM patients with neuropathy should consult with a neurologist and an oncologist who are both knowledgeable about WM. Proper diagnoses and beneficial treatments only result from a collaborative decision-making process between qualified physicians and the patient.

I am most grateful to have Dr. Luis Chu, my current oncologist at Florida Cancer Specialists in Sarasota. He is a compassionate human being and a skilled, humble physician who truly understands the complexities of WM. Also, I am appreciative of the tremendous kindness and knowledge of Dr. Jorge Castillo at the internationally renowned Bing Center for Waldenstrom's Macroglobulinemia at the Dana-Farber Cancer Institute. I visit Dr. Chu's office every six months and have my blood checked; in addition, I continue to consult with Dr. Castillo on an annual basis. I have great respect for both of my oncologists, and they have a wonderful, mutual respect for each other. I am indeed blessed by the Good Lord above!

Here's another truly amazing fact, given the rarity of this disease. I recently discovered that the International Waldenstrom's Macroglobulinemia Foundation (IWMF) office is located less than five miles from where I live in Sarasota. Of all the places I could have moved five years ago when I retired, I moved near the main office that provides

WM patients internationally with information and assistance. The IWMF web site is amazing.

When Arnold Smokler, a retired pharmacist in Sarasota, was diagnosed with WM, he could not find much information about this rare disease. So, in 1994, Arnold started a foundation in Sarasota to support those afflicted with Waldenstrom's macroglobulinemia and their family members. For over twenty years, the International Waldenstrom's Macroglobulinemia Foundation has grown tremendously, exerting a significant positive impact on the Waldenstrom's community worldwide!

The web site for the International Waldenstrom's Macroglobulinemia Foundation (www.iwmf.com), provides all types of available resources, including basic information about WM, lists of physicians, and other important data that may be particularly relevant to a patient or family members of a patient. This site is an invaluable resource to everyone affiliated with the WM community.

I only wish that I had known about the IWMF and the Dana-Farber Institute sooner. It is not always easy to begin wading through the often enigmatic pathway of understanding WM. Since it is a rare condition, I have discovered that my experience is not uncommon. Some oncologists may never even encounter any patients with WM throughout their entire careers. I took a somewhat circuitous path, but I finally did discover the resources and support system that are so vital to me, thanks be to God!

Since WM is so rare, it's been referred to as the "orphan disease" by many. However, tremendous strides have been made in funding, researching, and treating this disease just in the last three years. While there is no cure for WM, it is very treatable. I remain very optimistic about my health status. By pro-actively eating well, staying active, taking supplements, educating myself in every way possible, and, most importantly, praying, I hope to live many more productive years. I want to help educate others and give them reasons to be hopeful. I have been inspired by researchers, doctors, and patients I've met at conferences.

So, while I am on "watch and wait," sometimes I feel like I am sitting on the precipice of a storm cloud. Most of the time, I feel like I am sitting on the edge of a beautiful, nascent rainbow, waiting for all the lovely pastels to emerge in the sky. I am seeking that rainbow not only in *my* future, but also in the future for all Waldenstrom's patients. I wouldn't exchange anything I've experienced for the world! I have learned so much and have been deeply inspired by so many in the WM community. In my imagination, those rainbow colors are growing more vivid with each passing day. The brightness of those colors are elucidated by the knowledge I continue to accrue and the mutual support system I encounter on my daily WM journey.

Below are my lyrics to *Together, Forever Strong*, a song I am dedicating with love to everyone in the WM Family.

TOGETHER, FOREVER STRONG

Verse One:

> We greet the sunrise ev'ry day
> With dreams and goals that we all share.
> Just let that sunshine touch your face.
> With a smile you'll spread your love ev'rywhere.

Refrain:

> 'Cause we will walk together arm in arm
> As we fill our hearts with love and song.
> This is where we'll always proudly belong
> With these ties that bind us so tight.
> We're together forever strong;
> Yes, we're together forever strong.

Verse Two:

> So take my hand and we'll find our place
> Though the future is not always clear.
> But together there is nothing we can't face;
> With courage we can conquer our fears.

Refrain:

> 'Cause we will walk together arm in arm
> As we fill our hearts with love and song.
> This is where we'll always proudly belong
> With these ties that bind us so tight.
> We're together forever strong;
> Yes, we're together forever strong.

Bridge:

> Stay true to your convictions;
> Don't let the shadows of doubt creep in.
> Light up the world with your own vision.
> Step out of your box; don't be afraid!
> Be that spark that ignites a glist'ning flame of love!
> Just share the warmth of your love and let the world feel your love!!

Refrain:

> 'Cause we will walk together arm in arm
> As we fill our hearts with love and song.
> This is where we'll always proudly belong
> With these ties that bind us so tight.
> We're together forever strong;
> Yes, we're together forever strong.

Verse Three:

> If there comes a time when you're feelin' weak,
> You know we're here for you ev'ry day.
> And together we'll find the cure we seek.
> With hope in our hearts we will lead the way.

Refrain:

> 'Cause we will walk together arm in arm
> As we fill our hearts with love and song.

This is where we'll always proudly belong
With these ties that bind us so tight.
We're together forever strong;
Yes, we're together forever strong!
Yes, we're together forever strong!!
We're together forever strong!!!

CHAPTER TWO

A Different Perspective on Friday, the 13th

I T WAS A FRIDAY, THE 13TH- JUNE 13, 1958, to be exact. The priest carefully poured water over the forehead of the twelve-day-old infant girl as he proclaimed aloud, "I baptize you in the name of the Father, and of the Son, and of the Holy Spirit." The attentive Godmother tenderly held the baby as the Godfather, father, and the nurse from the hospital stood reverently in the background. You see, this was no ordinary Baptism!

When I was born, my mother was very critically ill. Peritonitis set in, her kidneys were shutting down; needless to say, things were "touch and go." And though, quite miraculously, I was born strong and healthy, (contrary to what the doctors had predicted,) it was decided that I would stay in the hospital an additional three weeks to help my mother heal both physically and psychologically. Yet this presented a slight dilemma with regards to my Baptism. Of course, if my well-being was in danger, then I could be baptized immediately at the hospital. However, that was not the case. Back in 1958, the priest baptized the baby in the church as soon as possible.

So, in stepped Reverend George Friel, O. P., a close family friend, a faithful Dominican priest, a well-respected professor at Providence College, and a colorful character, to say the least. Fr. Friel had a heart of gold, but he also was unafraid to speak up for any cause that he felt was just or to criticize any situation that he felt was unjust. So Fr. Friel approached the medical staff at the Women and Infants Hospital in Providence where I was born. He explained that he wanted to bring me to the local church to baptize me, and that this was an urgent matter. However, Father was emphatically told that under no circumstances could I leave the hospital and then return to be with my mother after being exposed to germs and viruses. After all, my mother spent time with me in the hospital every day, and nobody wanted her fragile immune system to be taxed. Still, Father Friel emphasized the transcendent importance of the Sacrament of Baptism.

As a result, the staff and Father reached a compromise. Father could take me to St. Pius Catholic Church, just a mile down the street from the hospital, and immediately baptize me there, as long as I was returned promptly to the hospital. To ensure that this would happen, the nursing supervisor attended my baptism, along with my Godparents, my father, and Father Friel. Father Friel had such a sense of humor that he baptized me "Anne Marie George," which is not only his first name, but my father's first name as well. I was whisked into the church, simply adorned in my diaper and undershirt, and then I was promptly whisked back to the hospital, with the nurse as my companion. This was the first time in the history of the hospital that something like this occurred. I guess you could say that my christening was both a sacred and historical event!

Father Friel, my parents, and my Godparents were always advocates for me, from my baptism as a twelve-day-old infant and throughout my entire life. My Godparents, Madeline and Harry Collins, were also my beloved aunt and uncle and were always an inspiration to me. They lived exemplary lives and loved me unconditionally. I never knew the name of the nurse, but I am grateful that she was understanding enough to make an exception to hospital rules and to attend my Baptism. I am happy to report that my mother made a full recovery and actually lived a generally strong, and healthy existence until February of 2014, just two months shy of her ninety-fourth birthday.

So while some associate Friday, the 13th with bad luck, I will always think of it as the most blessed day of my life. It was the day that I was baptized with the living waters of faith and initiated into the One, Holy, Catholic, and Apostolic Church, founded by Jesus Christ, Who is the Way, the Truth, and the Life. Everyone present at my Baptism has now passed on to the next world. I pray that they are enjoying the love, peace, and the pure bliss of heaven. I also hope someday to be standing by their side, gratefully sharing the joy of everlasting life with them.

CHAPTER THREE

Margie Fox and Smith Hill

W E COME IN ALL DIFFERENT SHADES! How about that!"
she thought to herself as she gazed around the classroom in total
amazement. It was the first time this shy four-year-old girl had seen other
little children her age who had a skin color that was much darker than hers.
"How neat is that!" she curiously pondered.

That day in 1962, Miss Fox, the beloved kindergarten teacher at
Berkshire St. School, invited a special guest to come visit her kindergarten
class. It was her niece, who was a bit shy, but also thrilled to have the honor
of visiting her aunt's class. When Miss Fox introduced her, the children all
looked at her with big smiles and admiration, like she was so lucky to have
such a "cool" aunt! She felt just as special as can be!

The friendly kindergarten teacher, Miss Fox, was sitting at the piano,
playing some favorite songs for her class of spellbound four- and five-year-
olds. They all loved Miss Fox. She had shiny, bright red hair and freckles,
reflective of her strong Irish heritage. Her father, John, had come into
Boston Harbor at the tender age of sixteen and then settled in Providence,
where he met and married her mother, Mary Ellen Murray. Marguerite
(or Margie as her family called her) was the eldest of the six daughters
in the Fox family. She remained single, devoting her life to teaching her
young kindergarten children, whom she loved, while also looking after her
mother, who had been widowed a few years back. The Berkshire Street
School where Marguerite taught, was located in the heart of Smith Hill,
not too far from the home where she grew up and where she still lived with
her mother.

Back in the twenties, when Margie and her five sisters were youngsters,
the neighborhood and surrounding community provided an environment

that was safe, welcoming, and pleasant. In fact, it was a lovely melting pot. People of different ethnic and religious backgrounds lived in a peaceful environment.

There were Armenian families, such as the Kazarian's. In fact, Harry Kazarian eventually became the Postmaster at the main post office in Providence. A few miles down the street was the ornate Armenian Apostolic Church, Saints Sahag and Mesrob, noted for the beautiful cross on the top. That cross still lights up in a gorgeous blue every night, hovering over the Downtown Providence skyline. Many families would stroll down the street to attend services there on a Sunday morning.

There were the McElroy's, the McGovern's, the Sullivan's, and, of course, the Fox family. The Irish families also could be seen strolling down to St. Patrick's Church on a Sunday morning, chatting and exhibiting their finery. The children and teen-agers would faithfully walk back and forth to St. Patrick's School in all kinds of weather.

On the next street over from the Fox family residence was Temple Beth David, a beautiful neighborhood synagogue. In fact, one of the Fox sisters, Regina, often would baby-sit for the rabbi's young children. Sometimes on a Saturday afternoon, she would bring them into St. Patrick's and ask them to quietly wait in the pew while she slipped into the Confessional. The Kessler family lived behind the Fox family; in fact, their backyards adjoined. There would be many great conversations whenever the laundry was being hung on the clothes line. Kessler's Bakery and Delicatessen was a wonderful place to sample delicious sandwiches and pastries.

A couple of blocks away there were devoted, hard-working Lithuanians such as the Kapiskas and Stoskus families who unwaveringly supported their church and the Smith Hill community. In fact, some of them helped to build St. Casimir's Church, brick by brick, with their bare hands.

So, you get the picture. In the first few decades of the twentieth century, everyone generally got along quite well in the close-knit Smith Hill neighborhood of Providence. They were all enthusiastically pursuing the American Dream and proud to become American citizens. Most of the families may not have had much in a material sense, having experienced the financial difficulties of the Depression; yet, what they *did* have was invaluable—a mutual concern and respect for one another. There was also an undeniable spiritual focus in the community, which, in my humble opinion, helped to unite everyone in an ecumenical manner.

Fast forward to the turbulent sixties. By this time, Smith Hill had evolved into more of an inner city community that was no longer as safe as it had once been. People now regularly locked their doors, and the police patrolled the area with much greater frequency. Still, the vast majority of people there were good, kind, and decent.

Margie Fox, the devoted kindergarten teacher, was no exception. Miss Fox invited her special guest to sit down with the class on the floor while she read her students a story. The guest sat down next to a beautiful African-American child who smiled warmly at her and immediately reached out to hold her hand—actually, my hand. Yes, Marguerite Fox was my beloved aunt, my mom's eldest sister, who introduced me to a wonderfully integrated group of children for the first time in my young life. I don't remember the name of the little girl who warmly smiled at me, but I'll always cherish her holding my hand and welcoming me with such innocence and acceptance.

I often think back to the day when I met that little girl with the smiling eyes, kind face, and loving gesture. To me, it epitomizes what Martin Luther King's dream is- for all children, black and white, and of every race, color, and creed, to hold hands in peace, love, and equality. On that fateful day in 1962 she and I were no longer strangers; instead we became fast friends.

My beloved aunt, or Auntie Margie as I called her, passed away on June 2, 1968, the day after my tenth birthday. However, she will always be in my heart and in the hearts of everyone who knew her, especially the students who were blessed to have her as a caring and devoted teacher.

I eventually became the music director at St. Casimir's Lithuanian Church from 1978 to 2007, and I was married there in 2008. I'm proud to say that my choir members adopted me as a fellow Lithuanian! In 1999, I spent about six months at St. Patrick's School, developing a middle school curriculum for teaching virtue and researching my doctoral dissertation. As I did my research and taught the students, I sat in the very same classroom where my mother sat as a first grader. Smith Hill still has left me with a rich legacy and continues to provide me with lifelong connections.

Pictured below are the six Fox sisters with their mother at Roger William Park
in Providence circa 1943. From left to right are Edna, Madeline, Mary,
Mary Ellen (my grandmother), Rita (my mother), Regina, and Margie
(the kindergarten teacher at Berkshire Street School).

This is a photo of my maternal grandfather, John Andrew Fox,
outside his neighborhood pub in Smith Hill.

CHAPTER FOUR

Our guardian angels were with my parents and me on this fateful day, for sure!

Illusions of Safety Shattered

I ENTERED THE HOUSE, spotted the mail on the floor directly below the slot in the front door and heard a rustling noise upstairs. It was a crisp, cold New England day in early December, my parents and I decided to do some Christmas shopping. I had just begun my semester break from college, and it was a beautiful clear day to be freely roaming about.

After a couple of hours of heavy-duty shopping, we hauled our shopping bags to the car and headed home, exhausted but satisfied with our purchases. On the way home, my parents offered to treat me to lunch at a local steakhouse. But since I wasn't terribly hungry and feeling a bit tired, I declined their generous offer. This was highly unusual for me, but we all decided to go directly home and rest for a bit.

I was the first to enter the house, and hearing the noise I quickly alerted my parents. My father, being the protector that he always was, cautioned my mom and me to just stay put while he went to investigate. He carefully inched his way up the winding staircase and suddenly stopped! He came flying down the stairs and told us in a frantic whisper to flee because an intruder had entered our home and might still be there!

Terrified, the three of us ran to our neighbor's home to call the police. I can remember my mom hyperventilating and barely able to speak. I just felt sort of numb. My father then described what he had witnessed at the top of the stairs. The linen closet at the end of the hallway was open and pillow cases were strewn on the floor. That was not a good sign, but we were all safe, thank God!

Two North Providence police officers arrived in a timely fashion. They quickly proceeded to thoroughly search the house from top to bottom, determining that nobody was there. In fact, the heavy thud that I heard was probably the intruder bounding out my upstairs bedroom window and making a quick escape by sliding down the roof above our back porch. There was a thin blanket of snow on the roof and some footprints were visible.

Well, the good news was that our time of arrival was impeccable. Evidently, the would-be thief had just started to open my mother's jewelry box, hoping to stuff the treasures he discovered into pillow cases. However, we arrived home just in the nick of time! Apparently, he simply dropped everything, quickly shoved open my bedroom window, and scampered away like a frightened squirrel.

But now the question was: "How did he enter our house in the first place?" Well, we had a cozy, screened-in back porch. That was our shelter and retreat during the warm summer months in Rhode Island. Between the porch and our dining room stood a quaint-looking door, painted in a lovely tone of aqua-blue, with several panes of glass. During the winter, I would often gaze through those panes of glass, reminiscing about the warm summer evenings we spent on that porch and eagerly anticipating the arrival of next summer. Evidently our intruder found that door to be inviting as well. After cutting the screen and entering the porch from our backyard, he shattered a pane of glass, reached around and simply unlocked the door from the inside. Our uninvited guest meandered through the house, discovered what he was looking for upstairs, and started to help himself.

Needless to say, on that fateful day, our illusions of safety were shattered. A solid wooden door with a dead bolt lock was installed. In fact, dead bolts were added to all the doors leading outside. Subsequently, an alarm system was installed.

If I had accepted my parents' offer for lunch, the results may have been catastrophic! Did we ever think that our little retreat, our lovely back porch, would become an entryway for a prospective thief to boldly follow?

Our guardian angels were with us that day in a very special way. After all, come to think of it, when did I ever refuse a steak dinner? Only God knows how often our guardian angels protect us, teach us discernment, and save us from danger.

CHAPTER FIVE

A Journey toward Marriage

C OULD THIS FINALLY BE THE RIGHT MAN FOR ME? I felt a sudden surge of expectation as his car pulled up next to mine in the local town hall parking lot that August 2, 2003. We had encountered one another at a Catholic singles web site. I suggested meeting at a central location that was easy to find since he lived about seventy miles away in a neighboring state. When I shook his hand, there was an earnest look in his eyes, accompanied by a boyish grin. He simply uttered, "Hi, I'm Mike." He sported a neatly trimmed moustache and was well groomed. His dark, wavy hair, friendly manner, infectious laughter, and down-to-earth temperament revealed sincerity.

It was definitely a very pleasant first meeting. We chatted easily while enjoying tasty sandwiches at a favorite local restaurant, followed by a vigorous walk. We shared our many common and diverse interests, our family backgrounds, and most importantly, our faith. And little did I think that a simple, routine ritual I performed in the midst of our first walk together would have such a profound and lasting impact on Mike and our relationship. As we were approaching the local Catholic Hospital, I immediately paused, took a right-hand turn, and proceeded toward the statue of Our Lady of Fatima, which is centrally located in front of Fatima Hospital. I simply commented that I never walk past that statue without stopping to pay the Blessed Mother a visit. This time, I made a silent prayer for Her intercession to the Lord, hoping that Mike might just be the one I'd been waiting a lifetime (forty-four years) for. Little did I realize that Mike had also been anticipating such a meeting for just about the same length of time!

This prayerful intercession to the Virgin Mary has become an on-going, integral aspect of our relationship. Only now, we share it together. In fact, attending Mass regularly, receiving the sacrament of Reconciliation, and praying the Rosary constitute the cornerstone of our bond with one another. As I sit here writing this reflection, it's been almost four years since that fateful day that we met. Mike and I became engaged on October 6, 2006, and we plan to be married in the Catholic Church on August 2, 2008—just a little over a year away and exactly five years from the date we first met.

Neither Mike nor I have ever been married before or have we ever experienced a serious relationship before. We both strongly value the importance of chastity, commitment, and fidelity to one another, to Church teaching, and most of all, to Our Sovereign Lord, Jesus Christ. I cherish Mike as a special gift I never dreamed I would receive. His meticulously recorded journal chronicles all the wonderful events in our lives together during the past four years. He continues to spend countless hours, writing his reflections on our love for the Lord and one another.

Mike's proposal to me was such a sacred event, filled with such tender surprises as he walked me to a lovely, neighborhood park, just across the street from Our Lady of Fatima Hospital. The dozen of white flowers planted nearby, symbolizing the purity in our relationship. The St. Raphael's medal he initially gave me, convincing me that this was merely a pre-engagement celebration, demonstrating our gratitude to the angel whose intercession also helped to bring us together. Then, the dozen of red roses also carefully planted amidst the trees, followed by Mike's humbly kneeling before me, presenting me with the most beautiful, sparkling diamond I had ever seen!

The proposal was followed by a romantic ride in a gondola on the Providence River, as our Venetian gondolier, Mario, serenaded us with "O Sole Mio" and "Santa Lucia." We then strolled along the historic streets of the East Side of Providence, indulging in scrumptious pastries at our favorite spot, the Meeting Street Café. That memorable night, October 6, 2006, (the eve of the Feast of Our Lady of the Rosary), culminated with the most sacred event of all—Mike and I reciting the Rosary together, praying with hearts full of gratitude and asking for God's continued blessings on our relationship and impending marriage.

I think back to the first time Mike and I strolled together and began to share our thoughts, dreams, and visions. I remember that silent intercessory prayer I murmured to Our Lady during our very first walk on August 2, 2003. Never in my wildest dreams could I have imagined such a heavenly response. Mike and I hope and pray that as we prepare for our special walk down the aisle and to the altar together at St. Casimir's Church on August 2, 2008, that we will continue to grow closer to God, to all members of God's family here on earth, and to one another. We want to help one another to attain eternal salvation to which we are all called. We pray that our lives as a Catholic couple will be a living testimony to God's graciousness and countless blessings! Nothing is impossible when we put our trust in God!

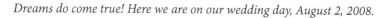

Dreams do come true! Here we are on our wedding day, August 2, 2008.

CHAPTER SIX

*My husband, Mike, is an absolute inspiration to all those who are privileged to
know him. He has overcome numerous obstacles throughout his life and
continues to transcend them with faith, love, and courage.*

Defying the Odds

O N APRIL FOOL'S DAY IN 1959, a brand new bundle of joy arrived in
the Vale household. This was number six, a vibrant infant son born
to Mary and Duke. His name was Michael Joseph. Right from the start,
Michael had tons of energy. That Mike was a real firecracker!

But Mary, his mom, started to notice that Mike's eyes did not seem to
follow movements in a normal fashion. Sure enough, the ophthalmologist
confirmed that Mike's eyes could not focus properly; he was actually cross-
eyed.

When Mike was five years of age, he had eye surgery to correct this
problem. However, while the vision in his left eye greatly improved, he
completely lost the vision in his right eye. Evidently, in 1964, that was the
best the doctor could do, and Mike accepted his fate with bravery and
determination. In fact, many other challenges would lie ahead for Mike.

One day in first grade, Mike suddenly put his head down on the
desk. Being known as a notorious little rascal, his teacher immediately
admonished him for seeking attention. "Mike, stop playing games and sit
up straight in your chair!" the teacher exclaimed. But when Mike made no
response and abruptly fell to the floor, she knew something was terribly
wrong.

It turned out that Mike was having a *grand mal* seizure, the first of many
he would experience for the next several years. The doctors diagnosed him

with epilepsy. After five long years of doctors' appointments, an extended stay in Boston's Kennedy Memorial Hospital, and trying a variety of medications, the seizures finally stopped in 1970.

Still, the voices of doubt and the naysayers he's encountered in life have probably been the greatest obstacles that Mike has overcome. Nonetheless, when he hears those voices in his head persuading him to just give in and accept mediocrity, he yells, "No way!"

For example there were those who warned him, "You'll never drive!" Yet, he's been driving for more than thirty years!

Instead of allowing his physical challenges to define him, Mike overcomes them by learning to adapt. There's no such thing as an "impossible dream" to Mike. He's learned to channel his emotions into vehicles of expression that many others in his situation would never even consider. Perhaps his most dramatic accomplishment came to fruition as he was approaching his forties.

For many years, Mike grappled with the idea of fulfilling a dream that would mean the world to him. Again and again, he deeply contemplated his desire to study photography.

The very rational, safe side of Mike's brain kept emphasizing certain limitations: *You're half blind; you don't have the necessary educational background; you're working full-time and don't have enough time to go to school; and, you're essentially crazy to even consider applying to photography school in the first place!*

Yet, the adventurous, risk-taking side of Mike's brain kept protesting and arguing with his more cautious side: *Your left eye has good vision; your ever-burgeoning passion for photography will spur you on to great accomplishments; you'll find the time no matter what your work schedule is; and, just go ahead and apply to the New England School of Photography!*

Well, I'm sure you can guess which side won out! In June of 2000, Mike attended his commencement ceremony at the prestigious New England School of Photography and received his diploma with pride. Did I mention that all the professors on his jury committee unanimously approved of his photography portfolio? Yes, Mike can jubilantly proclaim that he's a graduate of a renowned school of photography- a task that many of us with 20/20 vision could never accomplish.

Now fast forward another ten years. In May of 2010, a tumor was found on Mike's kidney. The urologist announced that the kidney must be unequivocally removed. Did Mike blithely accept that fate? Not a chance! It was not until he saw the third urologist that Mike reached a decision. Dr. Robert Carey, a nationally prominent urologist in Sarasota, stated that he would try to save the kidney, though the tumor was in a precarious location. With the utmost confidence, Mike gave the go-ahead for the delicate robotic surgery. Fortunately, the tumor was removed; the kidney was saved; and, Mike has been cancer free ever since, thanks to the good Lord above and to the skillful expertise of Dr. Carey!

The so-called "experts" predicted that Mike would have to settle for a limited quality of life, but he would not listen to those naysayers or those insidious little voices in his head. With the help of God and Mike's strong determination, I am confident that he will continue to thrive and adjust to whatever comes his way. Sometimes Mike can be as stubborn as a mule, but that persevering attitude has brought him much success. In fact, his faith, courage, and motivation to achieve continue to inspire everyone who is privileged to know him.

If you ever go to the drum circle at Casey Key in Nokomis or Siesta Key in Sarasota, Florida, you'll undoubtedly see Mike darting back and forth, taking awesome action shots of drummers, dancers, and spectators. Yes, Mike's a very special man!

This photo was taken by Cathy Ott Geisen, a dancer and devoted member of the Nokomis Drum Circle family.

CHAPTER SEVEN

A Most Incredible Mother

R ITA FRANCIS (FOX) McDONNELL was only capable of giving birth to me; in fact, she literally almost gave her life for me. My mom was extremely ill throughout her pregnancy. All the doctors told her that she could never give birth at all, due to large fibroid tumors in her uterus. Yet, God had other plans.

My mom and my dad were people of deep faith. They made a pilgrimage to the St. Anne de Beaupre Shrine in Canada, with the intention of petitioning for a child. I believe that God answers prayers in miraculous ways. It was His supernatural grace that transcended the natural expectations of my mother's physicians. The doctors repeatedly told my mother to just expect a miscarriage. Yet, the Good Lord had other plans. I came into this world as a strong, healthy baby on June 1, 1958. The doctors declared that I was a miracle! My mother came very close to death, but God, in His infinite mercy, pulled her through.

Mom was born on April 23, 1920 and always proudly proclaimed that Shirley Temple Black and William Shakespeare were also born on the twenty-third of April. During her ninety years on this earth, my mother accomplished many wonderful things, though she always gives all the glory to God.

As a devout Catholic, she attended Mass every day of her life until her health no longer permitted her to do so. Her faithfulness and unconditional love toward her devoted husband, George, was amazing. As her only daughter, I feel blessed beyond description. She was always a mentor, advisor, protector, and overall most incredible mother.

Having grown up during the Depression, she and her five sisters experienced difficult times. Yet, the love of her parents and her siblings bonded them closely. My mom was always the one that everyone depended upon. Even as the fifth child of six girls, she often ran the family errands and offered moral support whenever it was needed. Throughout her life, she continued to be the one that all of her sisters looked to for guidance. Rita always displayed a maternal, nurturing instinct.

Rita had a special affinity for children. In fact, she was like a surrogate mom to countless children through the years. When I was enrolled in a Catholic elementary school, she would voluntarily supervise children at lunchtime and recess. She also taught Catechism, always giving the children presents and inviting them to our house. When I became an elementary classroom teacher, she volunteered for many years at the school where I taught, even up into her mid-eighties, helping to tutor the primary grade students in math and reading skills.

When Rita fell and broke her hip in October of 2009, it was a bleak time. Yet, all the friends she had been supportive of came together and encouraged her to heal and return to her jovial self. Rita possessed an infectious, hearty laugh which everyone positively loved. On Friday, April 23, 2010, we all joyfully celebrated my mom's ninetieth birthday. She stood tall and proud, and I stood next to her, feeling so blessed!

This was a tender moment from Mom's ninetieth birthday celebration.

CHAPTER EIGHT

Disney, Dementia, and Dignity

I T WAS *MARY POPPINS* that became meaningful to my mother during her final years on this earth. It was the first movie my parents took me to see when I was in the first grade. I was enchanted and mesmerized by the animation, special effects, and heartwarming story. At the time, I never could have predicted how important *Mary Poppins* would become to my mother many years later.

Supercalifragilisticexpialidocious became one of her favorite words! Not only could she pronounce this multi-syllabic word flawlessly; she could also spell it! Being innately musical, she could sing the melody to this classic song perfectly in tune. Needless to say, I would sing and play this song whenever she was in the audience at the assisted living facility or nursing home. In fact, I still perform it frequently, always reminding the audience that it's a special song dedicated to my mom's memory. Mary Poppins would be proud. And so would Mom!

As my mother entered the early stages of dementia, she developed some brilliant coping strategies and defense mechanisms to accommodate her new reality. Throughout her life, my mother's memory was impeccable and her intellectual capabilities were quite exceptional as well. So, in order to retain a sense of dignity and self-respect, she would use certain verbal expressions that were especially meaningful to her. Speaking and singing specifically chosen words or phrases not only gave her a true sense of security and pride, it also provided her with a channel of expression that impressed others and endeared her to them.

In 1936, my mother, at the tender age of sixteen, graduated from St. Patrick's High School, located in Providence, Rhode Island. She was very proud of her Irish heritage and loved to share that fact with everyone!

However, what also became evident as she approached the age of ninety is that she was extremely proud of her ability to speak a few basic words in French. She studied French in high school and wanted everyone to know it! Yet, if someone posed the question, "*Parlez- vous francais?*" she would modestly reply, "*Un peu.*" (Just a little.) Her absolute favorite expression was "*Merci beaucoup!*" In fact, her nickname became *Merci Beaucoup*! She never failed to let everyone around her know that she learned these French expressions back in her high school days in the early thirties. Being able to say a few words in a foreign language boosted my mom's self-esteem and endeared her to all her caregivers and many friends. She never failed to show her caregivers a deep sense of appreciation, with a sincere, heartfelt sense of gratitude (whether she spoke in English or French.) Yet, more often than not, it was "Merci beaucoup!")

Mom also took great pride in becoming the resident spelling bee winner at Live Oak Manor, the wonderful assisted living facility where she lived with my father. Whenever an employee, a fellow resident, or even a visitor had trouble spelling a word, Rita always came to the rescue!

Besides "Supercalifragilisticexpialidocious," my mom had another favorite song. You might say that she stole it unabashedly from one of her contemporaries. She absolutely fell in love with Doris Day's theme song, "Que Sera, Sera" and seemed to adopt it as her very own theme song. I think what my mother really cherished most about this song was the lyrical phrase, "*Whatever will be, will be. The future's not ours to see…*" In fact, she usually sang the first couple of phrases of the song exclusively.

Yes, Rita was a wise and philosophical woman. She was also a woman of tremendous faith. I think she truly realized, deep down, that she had entered the stage in her life where she had to gradually surrender her independence and self-sufficiency to the responsibility of her compassionate caregivers and ultimately to the Good Lord, who would soon be calling her home.

Mom endured some losses in her final years: her agility as a line dancer, her ability to walk independently, the company of her five dearly departed sisters whom she deeply loved, her once stellar memory, and, of course, her biggest loss, my father, George (her husband of fifty-six years.) Still, I am confident that she had a joyful reunion with him in Paradise just nine weeks later. I am sure it was and will be a happy one for all eternity. So, "*Merci beaucoup*, Mom, for all the *Supercalifragilisticexpialidocious* lessons you taught me and the wonderful legacy you left behind."

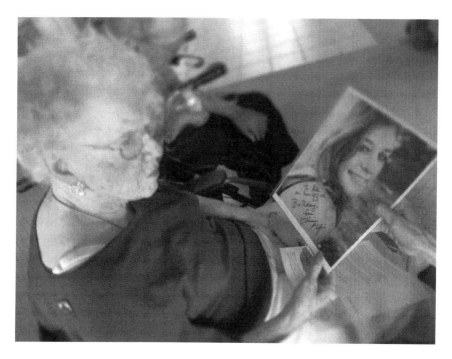

Louise Goffin kindly recorded my song, "Passing the Torch" as a present for Mom's ninety-third (final) birthday. It is a tribute to my grandfather, John Fox, who came to America from Ireland as a teen-ager. The lyrics are below.

PASSING THE TORCH

Sailing across the blue ocean they came with their worries and woes and cares,
Wondering just what would await them ashore as they left their homeland in tears.
Their hopes and dreams and all their fears were locked within their souls.

All bravely asked for the help of the Lord as they traveled through stormy
  seas.
Trust and devotion united each one as they clasped hands on bended
  knees.
And with their faith and dignity they faced each future day. God bless the
  USA!

Their sense of courage remains in my heart as if they were here by my
  side.
Such a commitment to greet the unknown as they worked to achieve with
  pride.
As time goes by, I wonder why they overcame such strife;
Yet, they simply cherished life.

Precious gifts were bequeathed to me like threads of continuity.
Yes, a long path of footsteps there will be for me to follow gratefully.

CHAPTER NINE

My Own Personal Time Machine

T HIS CHAIR WAS VERY PLAIN-LOOKING and ordinary- nothing aesthetically pleasing about it. It was just purely functional. It was a simple wooden chair with wooden arms and a cushion. It could turn into a reasonably comfortable lounge chair if necessary. I don't even remember if the cushion was brown or green. All I know is that it served its purpose. I occupied that chair for almost seventy-two continuous hours.

Yet it's what this chair signifies for me that will always be etched in my memory. It became my own personal time machine, a vehicle that transported me back to the age of five and then, in no particular chronological order, gradually brought me back to the present and the profound reality of what I was now confronting. While I sat in that chair, a whirlwind of memories that I had evidently neatly preserved way back in the recesses of my mind quickly rushed to the forefront with an overwhelming force!

For most of the time while I sat in that rather unattractive, yet useful chair, my laptop computer was in front of me. Just as my chair became my time machine transporter, my laptop became my navigator- assisting me in the retrieval of so many memories.

You see, what made this whole experience so moving to me was the person who was lying quietly in the bed next to where I was sitting. It was my beloved mom, Rita, the person who gave me life and who guided my life in so many significant ways. She just peacefully lay there, with her eyes closed. I didn't know how much longer her physical presence would be with me, but I sensed that it would not be very long. So I decided that no matter what the duration would be, I would sit by her side for the rest of the hours or days that she was on this earth. I would show her my love, devotion, and gratitude in any way I possibly could.

I suddenly had so many different flashbacks of fond memories, and I wanted so badly to somehow relive them with her in some tangible way. So I just started navigating the World Wide Web to retrieve musical memories that I could share with my mother. Even though she didn't speak, I was quite sure she could hear. My mom was never a professional musician, but she was indeed innately musical and always loved music. I remember at the age of four or five, I'd listen to her sing song after song, and I just started to naturally harmonize with her.

One of my first stops on the World Wide Web was Spotify. I soon found Nat King Cole singing "Rambling Rose," remembering how she played that record over and over and how excited she was to go with my dad to see Nat perform in the early sixties. Next, it was Dean Martin singing "Everybody Loves Somebody Sometimes." Of course, I simply *had* to play John McCormack, singing the classic Irish tunes. I so vividly recalled her playing those Irish songs on the record player again and again when I was a young child. And then I discovered Doris Day singing "Que Sera, Sera," another song that recently became a favorite of my mom's. I suddenly became my mother's personal deejay, sitting in the chair beside her bed, commenting on the personal significance of every song.

Another treasure trove was discovered at hulu.com. There I found so many classic episodes of *I Love Lucy* and *The Lucy Show*, which we both always loved to watch together. Finally, I discovered her all-time favorite TV show, *The Lawrence Welk Show*. Every Saturday night, year after year, my mother sat in front of the television set, simply mesmerized by Lawrence Welk, his orchestra, and all the talented musicians performing a variety of musical styles from her era.

Intermittently, between the music and TV shows I discovered on-line, I visited the web site for the Global Catholic Network- EWTN. The Eternal Word Television Network (EWTN) was my mom's absolute favorite cable channel when she lived in Rhode Island. She loved all the inspirational programs. She faithfully attended daily Mass with my father for as long as her health allowed. When my mom could no longer attend Mass every day, her link to God and her faith became EWTN. This time,

I visited the EWTN web site and played mp3 files of the Sisters reciting the Rosary and the Divine Mercy Chaplet, prayers that she was devoted to throughout her life.

After the first forty-eight hours had passed, I sat upright in my chair and opened Microsoft Word on my laptop. I then began to gradually compose my mom's obituary. I wanted to share the story of her life in a loving and comprehensive way.

When I wasn't navigating the World Wide Web, typing bits and pieces of my mom's obituary, and reflecting about the awe-inspiring life she led, I sat quietly in that chair, praying for her to have a peaceful passing. I also prayed for the courage to cope with another loss after just losing my dad within the last two months. My devoted husband, Mike, as well as many staff members, stopped by to check on me from time to time and bring me food or just give me a hug. The staff at the Palmer Ranch Nursing Facility in Sarasota provided my mom with outstanding, loving care, and I will be forever grateful for that.

Tuesday evening rolled around. With the exception of going to Mass Saturday night and taking a shower on Monday, I essentially had been by my mom's side since early Saturday morning, sitting in that chair- the chair that became my physical support and temporary shelter from the world.

All of a sudden, sometime between eight and nine o'clock Tuesday night, her eyes opened wide- and I mean, wide! She actually kept them open! I was so excited because my mother literally had not opened her eyes for more than a few brief moments in almost two months. At the same time, she started to perspire profusely and struggle a bit more with her breathing. So, I called my husband, Mike, and asked him to come and keep a bedside vigil with me. I think she suddenly knew that she was on her way to heaven to be reunited with her beloved husband, George.

Now, I was able to move my laptop to her bed! I could actually show her episodes of Lawrence Welk! I'm not sure if any of this really registered with her nor not, but she appeared to be looking at the screen. Perhaps it was just that God, in His mercy, knew how important it was for me to make eye contact with my mom and tell her how much she meant to me before she departed from this world. My husband took advantage of that same opportunity to look lovingly into my mom's eyes and reassure her that he'd always take care of me.

Amazingly, even when she took her last peaceful breath around quarter past three on the morning of February 18, 2014, her eyes still remained wide open. So, finally Mom had made the ultimate journey to eternal life. No more pain and suffering- just inexplicable joy and peace! No chairs or beds needed when you are before the throne of God! I can envision her spirit flying freely while she sings with the choir of angels.

Two months after my mom passed away, I found a card in her old, tattered prayer book. It was a memorial prayer card for her father, John A. Fox. As I looked at this card from 1960, I couldn't believe what I saw! My maternal grandfather entered eternal life on the same date that his loving daughter, Rita, did- February 18th! My final birthday gift to my mom on April 23, 2013 was a special song I had composed in memory of her dad. She was so proud of that song! I can't help but think that her father was there at the pearly gates to welcome his daughter with open arms and usher her into heaven. He had been patiently waiting to welcome her for exactly fifty-four years!!

A simple chair, accompanied by a laptop, both anchored me and transported me through time. The laptop was my navigator in many ways, but that chair supported me. Figuratively speaking, it was a vehicle to transport me through the memories of the last five decades of my life with Mom. Practically speaking, I ate in that chair, slept in that chair, and typed my mom's meaningful life story in that chair. Most importantly, during the last several hours of my mom's almost ninety-four years on this earth, I held her hand and expressed my unconditional love and appreciation for her in that chair. I'll always remember and cherish sitting in that very ordinary chair for many extraordinary reasons. It really did become my own personal time machine!

This is the last photo taken of my mother and me together.
It was Christmas Day, 2013.

CHAPTER TEN

This is a poetic tribute to my loving husband, Mike.

TRANSFORMING A YOUNG BOY'S LIFE

A zealous boy at age eleven-
The youngest of six, a gift from heaven.
Adored by his parents and siblings, for sure.
In the Vale family household he caused quite a stir!

Mike's boundless energy and sense of adventure
Were dampened a bit when he had his first seizure.
His vision was limited to the left eye only;
Blindness and epilepsy can make a boy feel lonely.

Yet, Mike's spirit of sheer determination
Has always transcended his physical limitations.
And when Mike met the Franciscan Missionaries of Mary,
Their compassion would lighten the burdens he carried.

The kind-hearted teachers, nurses, and nuns
Made many activities both novel and fun!
Their love touched Mike in a most profound way.
"That was the best year of my life!" he'll frequently say.

There were lessons to be taught in discipline and sharing.
Mike learned about humility, gentleness, and caring.
At the end of each weekend he'd leave Mom and Dad;
Still, this was no infirmary; it was another family he now had.

Mike displayed creativity while painting a scene, alas!
He discovered this latent talent while attending art class.
He also joined the hospital troop of Cub Scouts,
Taking pride in his membership and uniform, no doubt.

Sneakily, Mike dashed through the halls with lightning speed.
He'd throw caution to the wind and pay the rules no heed!
He was a typical boy who thrived on activity.
And when it came to mischief he showed some proclivity.

One day, Mike and a friend had immediately seen
A tempting, well-stocked candy machine.
When their coins were inserted, packs of gum exploded!
They hit the jackpot, for sure, and their pockets were loaded!

Yet, when a staff member learned of their new-found treasure,
They had to relinquish it all in good measure.
Honesty, integrity, justice, and truth
Were the Franciscan values Mike learned well as a youth.

Sunday night's home departures were tinged with sadness
Yet, returning to the hospital brought Mike a jolt of gladness!
A kind-hearted gentleman, who was a volunteer
Took Mike under his wing as soon as he'd appear.

Along the side of the shower stall was a sturdy bar
That reached quite high and extended rather far.
So there Mike would swing like a monkey on a limb
While the kind-hearted man would stand by to catch him.

Mike compares his experience to being at camp.
As he rambunctiously pushed his friend down the wheelchair ramp,
The accelerating speed would eventually propel
His friend from the wheelchair as he accidentally fell.

Thank God his buddy was not hurt bad.
Mike learned a valuable lesson and felt very sad.
But the staff was always there to teach him moderation,
And for that Mike will forever express appreciation.

Running freely in the hospital playground
With an intense energy and joy that abounds
Mike vigorously tossed a Frisbee in the sky,
Which landed on the hospital roof; that was quite high!

Mike tried to climb the drain pipe to retrieve it
'Til he was sternly instructed to get down and just leave it.
Mike's always been quite feisty and inquisitive,
Yet, he's also understanding, kind, and sensitive.

Mike vividly recalls an Irish C. N. A.
Who, with her lilting brogue and charming way,
Gave Mike an actual brick of the "Old Sod,"
And his eyes lit up like a lighthouse on Cape Cod!

Kennedy Memorial (now Franciscan) Hospital became
The shelter from a world where fortune and fame
Are often sought exclusively in self-serving ways.
Yet, true to its vision, this children's hospital stays.

Mike gradually experienced a true liberation
From the inferior feelings threatening the integration
Of his entire body, soul, and mind.
The Franciscan ministry is indeed a rare find!

In the hospital chapel all gathered in celebration
As Mike was administered the Sacrament of Confirmation.
And as he faithfully served Mass at the chapel's altar,
His Catholicism was reaffirmed with no trace of falter.

In 1970, Mike's grand mal seizures ceased.
We thank God every day and are extremely pleased.
That year Franciscan Hospital came to Mike's aid.
It was an experience of a lifetime that he'll never trade.

Despite life's challenges, Mike's learned to succeed.
He's been steadily employed and always met his own needs.
The next fact is amazing to this biographer,
But Mike, despite his blindness, is a professional photographer!

There were times in Mike's life that were quite dismal, or so it seemed;
But, the lessons he learned at Franciscan Hospital taught him to dream:
To persevere, to work hard, and to stay close to the Lord,
And in those lessons, as Mike's wife, I share in full accord.

On the next page is a photo of Mike in May of 1970. He was all dressed up with a suit and tie, loyally standing behind his buddy, Gabriel, outside the Kennedy Memorial Hospital chapel on their Confirmation day.

PART II
Tokens of Appreciation

CHAPTER ELEVEN

Time Passages

Ah, if we could only hop aboard a time machine and be transported to any era we'd probably be absolutely astonished at what we might experience! Or even if we could instantaneously visit the past or fast forward to any time in our own lives, our perceptions of that moment in time may pleasantly surprise us.

In April of 2015, my husband, Mike, and I entered the Franciscan Hospital for Children in Brighton, Massachusetts. It had been forty-five years since Mike had happily interacted with the compassionate staff and terrific friends he met there. He had been a resident at what was then called Kennedy Memorial Hospital (now Franciscan Hospital for Children) for one year and still considers that year to be the best of his childhood, perhaps even the best year of his entire life! Many things had changed in terms of the building's structure and the particular services being offered, but some things remained exactly the same. Above all, the compassionate care provided there and the supportive outreach to and from the surrounding community are still very evident.

Mike entered the Franciscan Hospital in 1969 as a shy, introverted boy who was lacking self-confidence. He felt somewhat isolated and disengaged in school because his epileptic seizures were still uncontrolled, and consequently he was unable to attend school regularly like other children. Also, learning to read and write was more of a challenge since he had no vision in his right eye. However, after one year, Mike left the hospital feeling better about himself, and more importantly, never again experiencing any seizures! Though he still had many challenges ahead of him, he now felt more confident about not only facing those challenges, but transcending them.

Fast forward to April 21, 2015. This time, Mike entered Franciscan Hospital, full of eager anticipation and confidence, with his wife, yours truly, by his side. We checked in with the receptionist who asked us to be seated for a few minutes while we waited for our tour to begin.

All of a sudden, the elevator doors opened, and a distinguished-looking gentleman and two lovely ladies (with one holding a camera) rushed over to Mike to shake his hand and to give him a hearty welcome. The kind gentleman who humbly introduced himself as "John" just happens to be John D. Nash, the President and CEO of Franciscan Hospital for Children. He was even holding the hand-written note of inquiry we had mailed several weeks ago! Several photographs of Mike and Mr. Nash were taken to permanently preserve this special encounter in our memories for many years to come. Mike was indeed welcomed back in an extraordinary way and congratulated heartily for how well he has done in overcoming the challenges he has encountered throughout his life. We are sincerely touched and grateful that Mr. Nash took time from his busy schedule to personally greet us.

Our tour was wonderful and brought back so many fond memories for Mike! We would like to commend the kind and competent Deanna Dwyer, who coordinated our visit, and the equally personable and capable Chantal Brandimarte, who gave us a most enjoyable tour of the hospital. These lovely ladies did a superb job!

Mike and I have happily discovered that reunions are held periodically at the hospital. We hope that this initial visit is just the beginning of a wonderful journey of sweet reminiscing for Mike, as well as a new journey on which we can embark together. Mike is now hoping to reconnect with others who were at Franciscan Hospital when he was a patient there. We both hope to visit again in the future and to give back to the hospital in any way that we can.

Mike emerged from the Franciscan Hospital in 1970 as a more confident eleven-year-old boy, seizure-free, who was ready to overcome his future challenges with determination. Ever true to his convictions, forty-five years later and still seizure-free, Mike returned to the hospital as a mature, compassionate, successful member of society, devoted to the Lord, his wife, and his community.

Mike and I are most grateful to this incredible children's hospital and the role its staff played in transforming the life of a young boy.

Today, there is still a young boy deep inside Mike, my amazing husband, who will remain ever grateful for the transformation he experienced forty-five years ago at Franciscan Hospital for Children. There is no doubt that this outstanding medical facility in Brighton, Massachusetts truly remains a beacon of hope for children with special needs and for their families worldwide.

Mike and I are pictured here with John Nash, the CEO of Franciscan Children's Hospital, during our visit to the hospital in April of 2015, forty-five years after Mike was a resident there. We are most grateful to Mr. Nash and his wonderful staff for their warmth and kind hospitality in making us both feel so welcome!

CHAPTER TWELVE

ODE TO THE FEISTY ONE!

You were a feisty little tyke,
You little rascal, Mike!
That was a nickname well deserved
From what we all observed!
Though you're still as feisty as hell,
There's so much more to tell.

You've never failed to persevere;
Faith takes the place of any fear.
Even as a young patient in Brighton,
You continued to amaze and enlighten.
You gratefully accepted a coloring book
And such kindness you never, ever forsook.

It was Uncle Jim who was humbly involved;
It took a while before the mystery was solved.
He was unassumingly driving by
And quietly slipped you a gift, but why?
He saw something special in his sister's son;
He certainly was not the only one!

My mom and you had lots of fun;
In fact, you were like her adopted son.
Yet, my mom, with respect, dignity, and grace,
Always said she'd never take your mom's place.

The two of you loved to mutually tease;
Still, in Mom's final weeks you were there to appease.

As she sadly declined how you'd valiantly strive
To feed sweet Rita, just to keep her alive!
You whispered "I love you" so softly in her ear
As she entered into Paradise in her ninety-third year.
You promised her you'd take care of me always.
That includes all the rest of my God-ordained days.

As we were leaving Dad at the end of the day,
"I love you both" is what he would say.
When my father lay dying in the ICU,
You said, "Don't worry, George. Anne's mine, too.
I love you, George. I'll care for Anne Marie.
Go in peace; my wife she'll always be."

And Mike, you never forgot Uncle Jim's gift of love.
You returned it to him; he's smiling from above.
When your beloved uncle passed away,
Near the casket, a special mug was on display.
It was the MTA mug you designed for Uncle Jim.
It will be a lasting, loving remembrance of him.

Your feisty nature has kept everyone on their toes!
Still, your tender side is reflected in decades of photos.
Every Murphy-Vale event that's ever been mapped
Is recorded for posterity in the pictures you've snapped.
Mike, you've matured into a loving, kind man;
We were likewise blessed when you joined the McDonnell clan.

I am so proud of Mike. He's an inspiration to all who are privileged to know him. Here we are at Casey Key Beach in Nokomis, FL on the Fourth of July!

CHAPTER THIRTEEN

Sharing a Cup of Tea

A TRULY FULFILLING LIFE IS LIKE A TEA CUP filled with a full-bodied, aromatic tea. One that is both soothing and relaxing with each sip and rejuvenating in taste and flavor.

Enjoying such a cup of tea every evening is a ritual my husband and I enjoy together. Every night at quarter to ten, my husband, Mike, makes me a cup of tea. He usually infuses my favorite flavor, which is a luscious blend of cinnamon and chai. As we enjoy our tea together we often either watch television together or reflect on our day. We may even discuss future plans or enjoy a favorite movie on a DVD.

We don't own a mansion or have our own personal assistants at our beckon call, but we have each other. Even with the normal ups and downs that we may experience in our relationship, we try to prioritize our faith and our commitment to each other, relegating our material possessions to a lower level of significance At the end of the day, sipping from a tea cup filled with soothing, rich tea that we each savor together is a simple, cherished experience. It's much better than being alone in a mansion, shedding copious tears, perhaps enough to fill an empty tea cup.

Yes, it's possible to have fame and fortune, as well as a truly fulfilling life. Still, in that case, I think it's more of a challenge to balance everything. I'll take a delicious cup of tea, lovingly made by my husband any day over fame and fortune. To me, our tea time is priceless.

CHAPTER FOURTEEN

Drumming Together and Gazing Upward

I's THE MIDDLE OF THE WEEK—Wednesday, to be exact! We're standing in a loving circle of humanity, feeling the lovely grains of sand at our feet and the warmth of love in our souls, as we participate in our drum circle at Casey Key in Nokomis.

Women, men, and children inside the circle are dancing, jumping, smiling, and playing tambourines. We drummers are playing congas, bongos, djembes, and all sorts of drums- all sizes and shapes, ranging from the booming of a very low-pitched bass drum, which is the heartbeat of the percussion ensemble, to the high-pitched sounds of jingling bells. You can just feel the excitement in every muscle of your body and with every beat of your heart.

There's a slight breeze, but the beaming sun is shining down on us in its usual implacable manner on a typical summer evening in Southwest Florida. The intensity of our motions is reflected in the beads of sweat forming on our brows, eventually becoming streams of sweat adorning our faces, necks, and backs.

Time passes so quickly. After a couple of hours fly by, the sky beings to display a glowing, reddish tint, so serene to behold. The suns starts to fade and sink down ever so gradually, almost imperceptibly.

Just as the sun is about to set, the energy of our drumming and the propulsion of the dancers' movement changes with an ever-increasing tempo and intensity. In fact, the percussive propensity in the circle reaches a fever pitch and is only matched by the solar energy that is about to descend and disappear into the horizon.

Finally, the sun sets with great fanfare, and we all collectively take our last gasp of breath as we take a welcome break. We cease the incredible momentum, we applaud, and we gaze in awe at the majesty of the sky. Thanks be to God, the sun has set on another beautiful day in Southwest Florida.

Once we become rejuvenated, we joyfully resume our drumming for the remainder of the evening, feeling refreshed by a slight breeze. Watching the sunset is always the pinnacle of our drum circle experience.

CHAPTER FIFTEEN

This is a tribute to my mother-in-law, Mary Vale, whom I never had the privilege of meeting. This is my account, based on interviews with my husband, Mike, and some of his siblings. Rest in peace, Mary.

ODE TO MARY MURPHY VALE

News about Mary escaped the front page,
But yet to all who knew her she was a true sage.
She didn't give lectures from coast to coast.
Her story wasn't captured in the Huffington Post.

Her life was never featured in the secular media;
Her biography's missing from Wikipedia.
She never was awarded a Pulitzer Prize;
Yet, her ideas were cogent and her words were wise.

She knew that *"Charity begins at home."*
Her love for family is acknowledged in this poem.
Her generous deeds spread near and far.
Everyone's needs were on Mary's radar!

Mary's Irish, smiling eyes and joy would reveal:
"What the eyes don't see, the heart can't feel!"
Her favorite quotes were reflected in her daily living,
Taking pride in her family and selflessly giving.

She admired acting legends like Bacall and Tracy
As she humbly did her chores while watching TV.
She shared the gift of humor with each daughter and son
And laughed out loud at their silly antics and fun!

She could never give enough in the name of the Lord.
She generously gave more than she could truly afford;
But hers was an eternal vision- not a worldly perspective.
She sought mercy over justice, unlike a mere detective.

Her quiet, joyful presence was always there.
She avoided the limelight or any fanfare.
Through every tribulation and trial,
She clung to the Cross and managed to smile.

Mary never sought any pity or attention.
Not a worry or pain or burden did she mention.
As the Virgin Mary stood at the Cross of Her Son,
She likewise grieved the death of her beloved one.

She endured the loss of her daughter, her namesake
For she knew that the Lord gives life and can also take
Back His children when we least expect.
This heavy burden she'd bravely accept.

As mother, wife, sister, or friend,
On Mary's loyalty you could always depend.
She frequented Confession and received the Holy Host.
She atoned for her sins; never did she boast.

Mary deeply valued her maternal vocation;
She showed her compassion with no hesitation.
She sought no fulfillment in a profession or career;
But to her family and friends, she was priceless and dear!

She showed no ego, but glorified her Creator.
She followed only the God Who had made her.
Mother Teresa said that faith, not success, would suffice;
So with confidence we pray that Mary's now in Paradise.

This is a photo of my kind-hearted mother-in-law, Mary Murphy Vale,
devoted wife of Anthony "Duke" Vale and proud mother of six children:
Peggy, Maureen, Dennis, Stephen, Mary, and Mike. She was also a loving
grandmother to several grandchildren who adored her.

CHAPTER SIXTEEN

FOREVER BY MY SIDE

My mom, Rita, was born in 1920.
Money was scarce and troubles were plenty.
But her faith was strong and her spirit was stoic.
In fact, I'd say she was heroic.

You'd be hard pressed to find
Someone who loved mankind
More than my beloved mother
Whose motto was "to love one another."

She was generous and beneficent,
Yet reserved and somewhat reticent.
You'd sense she wanted to express a bit more,
But was rather hesitant to open the door.

The Depression Era left its mark.
Her youthful days were sometimes dark.
But in those days you'd never reveal
Pain or heartache- you learned to conceal.

Mom was very bright and witty
Extremely dignified and really pretty.
Yes, Rita stood so proud and tall,
Possessing a memory that stunned us all!

Around the age of eighty-five
Mom's spirit was amazingly alive!
But her exceptional memory that was one-of-a-kind
Was showing some traces of lagging behind.

And yet there appeared a silver lining,
Defying description or even defining!
Suddenly, my reserved and often shy mother
Took on the ebullient nature of another!

Rita just lifted her protective mask
And it seemed to be an effortless task!
Her nature was no longer shy and coy.
It transformed overnight into boundless joy!

Though dementia can dissolve into sadness and tears,
And episodes, too, of stress and fear.
I choose to remember how out-going and free
My mom became- free to "be me!"

But Rita's carefree state would end
When she lost her husband and very best friend.
Yes, George, my beloved dad, was the true love of her life,
And his passing last December caused deep grief and strife.

Mom's eyes now closed – no facial expression.
The doctor called it a terminal depression.
Those once bright eyes might glimmer for a time,
But they now reflected no reason or rhyme.

For the next nine weeks, Rita barely spoke a word.
Though her eyes were shut, I'm sure that she heard
The love I'd express and the music I'd play;
But that mask of grief stayed day after day.

Yes, Rita so wanted to be with her George
And I prayed that God would quickly forge
A happy reunion between Mom and Dad.
To see Mom like this was just too sad!

Finally, one dark February night
Mom apparently saw the light!
All of a sudden, her eyes opened wide
While I expressed to her all I felt inside.

The mask had vanished as did her sorrow.
She now anticipated her new tomorrow.
We looked into each other's eyes 'til morn.
Rita knew she would soon be reborn.

And sure enough at three fifteen,
With eyes wide open and totally serene,
Rita peacefully entered eternity,
Joining George in blissful unity.

Mom and Dad are in the presence of the Lord
With the angels and saints in one accord.
No more earthly mask and nothing left to hide,
And though I miss seeing them, they're forever by my side.

My parents, George and Rita, will forever be by my side.

Here is a photo of my parents and me on my wedding day
in front of our former home in North Providence.

St. Casimir's is the church where I was music director for over thirty years. It is also the church where Mike and I were married on August 2, 2008.

My parents heartily welcomed guests in the foyer of St. Casimir's Church on my wedding day.

On May 11, 1957, my parents were married at St. Patrick's Church,
just a couple of blocks away from St. Casimir's.

Below are photos of Reverend James Ruggieri and Reverend T. J. Varghese
who con-celebrated our wedding liturgy.

Father James and Father Varghese are both humble servants of God and holy priests,
totally dedicated to their vocations. Father James is Pastor of St. Patrick's Church in
the Smith Hill section of Providence and Father Varghese is Pastor of St. Eugene's
Church in rural Glocester. Both of these devout priests offered great comfort to me
when my parents passed away. Father Varghese, who knew my parents very well,
celebrated their funeral liturgies. May God continue to bless Father James and Father
Varghese in their ministries as they serve others in His name.

CHAPTER SEVENTEEN

This is a memorial tribute to my special niece, Elizabeth Vale. During her twenty-one years on earth, she touched many lives in a truly profound manner. Her kindness and love will always be remembered.

ODE TO LIZ

Liz, this tribute to you is filled with love.
You continue to be a blessing from above.
Your myriad talents and selfless proclivity
Were always reflective of your warm sensitivity.
Your academic prowess was so extraordinary.
Your superior achievements as a writer were legendary.
Above all, shining through your plethora of gifts
Is your altruistic nature and desire to uplift
Everyone's spirits with your sweet tenderness.
Your good deeds were permeated with such kindness!
In trying circumstances you were brave and stoic.
Your perpetual concern for others was Christ-like and heroic.
You've been a beacon of light in your own unique way.
Your joyful smile and warm embrace brightened each day.
Though we miss your physical presence, your spirit is a part
Of the love you've indelibly imprinted in our memory and heart.

This is beautiful Liz Vale, with her adoring father, Steve.
Steve, Mike's brother, was a groomsman in our wedding.

CHAPTER EIGHTEEN

FIVE REFLECTIONS ON PEGGY, OUR *QUEEN FOR THE DAY*— *(A Seventieth Birthday Tribute)*

Who You Are:

>A perpetual student who takes time to discern,
>Who always shows others your utmost concern.
>With a quest for knowledge that's indeed rapacious;
>You're unequivocally perspicacious!

Your Humble Wishes:

>An intimate birthday celebration-
>No ostentatious coronation!
>Your desires reflect your humble style-
>A day to cherish family while…

What You Deserve:

>They show you just how much they care
>With heartfelt expressions of love and prayer,
>Showering you with attention you so richly deserve;
>Paying lofty compliments without reserve!

A Day Fit for a Queen:

>Another milestone to joyfully celebrate!
>Sit back, relax- no need to delegate.
>It's now your day to be treated like a queen!
>Just absorb this love and affection, and feel serene.

Future Wishes for You:

> Wishing you the best life offers in coming years,
> Enveloped by the love of family, those far and near.

Here is Peggy DeBoy dancing with her brother, Mike, on our wedding day.
She is a caring wife, mother, and grandmother. Peggy also taught at several
Catholic and public schools, including the RI School for the Deaf.

CHAPTER NINETEEN

Mike's sister, Maureen, is a talented baker, pastry artist, and owner of "The Cake Lady." This was my tribute to her on the occasion of her seventieth birthday.

A TRIBUTE TO MAUREEN,
"THE CAKE LADY"

What we admire most about you, Maureen,
Is your commitment and drive, while remaining serene.
You're always striving for true perfection
With every lovely, luscious confection!
Those of us who lack your inimitable skill
Appreciate your gifts, which are evolving still!

Nothing about you surprises me at all.
I'm an eye witness to your bungee jump at the mall!
The reserved among us might call that outrageous,
But I think that you're truly courageous!
Your sumptuous desserts are just sensational;
Your adventurous spirit is inspirational!

Though your talents are varied and most prolific,
It's your loyalty and strength that are really terrific.
There's a loving spirit that radiates from you
To all your friends and family who
Truly appreciate your kindness and concern
And the example you provide from which we learn.

Your constant love reveals warmth and stability
To each of us who marvel at your unique ability.
As a sister, mother, grandmother, and wife
You teach us what's really important in this life.
You give of yourself to everyone in need
With encouraging words and thoughtful deeds.

We are blessed to be part of your birthday celebration
As we jubilantly express our sincere congratulations!
During these wonderful seventy years
You've often laughed and shed some tears.
Yet, no matter what life brings your way
The love you exude still touches us each day!

Here is the "Cake Lady," Maureen Keefe, with her granddaughter, Jane Mailhiot.

CHAPTER TWENTY

A TRIBUTE TO OUR HERO, FIREFIGHTER TOM KEEFE

You're a true, genuine hero to others,
In a unique band of sisters and brothers.
You're strong, skilled, courageous, and daring;
Yet ever so gentle, supportive, and caring.
The distressed gratefully express heartfelt elation
While our unsung hero brings deep consolation.
"Our brave guardian angel nobly and swiftly came
To rescue us from danger and extinguish the flame!"
Now it's transformed into a flame of abiding love
Which will forever burn brightly in all our hearts.
Our unsung hero, guided by the Good Lord above,
Humbly, steadfastly, and devotedly does his part.
Indeed, God's special band of sisters and brothers
Who selflessly unite to heal, protect, and save others
Will always be cherished for serving God and mankind,
Tirelessly working to preserve body, spirit, and mind.
Thank you, Tom, for being a part of God's special band
And for your heroism, resonating throughout our land!

Here is Tom Keefe (Maureen's husband) and Mike's best man.
Tom is a generous, caring person.

CHAPTER TWENTY-ONE

This is a truly a whisper from above- a reassuring message. To this day, I'm
convinced that I heard Dad playing his trumpet, just for me!

COLOR ME SILVER AND RED:
LIFE'S INTERSECTING THREAD

A sparkling trumpet, shiny and silver
In a bright red stocking that Santa would deliver.
This was the toy I received Christmas Day
As I would press down the valves and pretend to play.
My dad would play with that *Big Band* sound.
Playing like his idol, Harry James, so renowned.

By the age of nine, I could play a real horn
So now the father-daughter duo was born!
We joyfully allowed music to brighten our day.
The occasions would change, but the music would stay.
There's nothing quite like a trumpet fanfare
To uplift one's mood and surely clear the air.

I recall the Easter Vigils with chanting so soft
As we watched the solemn processions from the church's choir loft.
After the extinguishing of the candles' flames
The lights came on and the "Gloria" was exclaimed.
As our shiny, silver trumpets would declare:
"Jesus is risen; He's present everywhere!"

I'd chuckle as I viewed awakenings so abrupt.
It sometimes seemed that the trumpets would interrupt
Some dozing congregants who succumbed to a nap.
But on Easter we should rejoice, sing aloud, and yes, clap!
It's funny the things that you recall out of the blue,
Not realizing at the time how they'll impact you.

I also recall Dad walking me up the aisle,
But this time another played his trumpet in style.
As I was leaving the church with my husband, Mike
That shiny, silver trumpet still sounded like
What I envision the angels' choirs must be-
The ones I hope to hear and see.

As the final strains of "Trumpet Tune" faded away,
We stood on the sidewalk with much to say
As we greeted all our family and friends.
But in an instant I feared that my world might end!
With no warning, Mom fainted, leaning against Dad,
As my emotions plummeted from ecstatic to sad.

Someone called 911 as quick as a wink
As I could feel my emotions suddenly sink.
After sipping some water, my mom came around!
All was OK; she was safe and sound.
We were told it was dehydration;
I felt such total relief and elation.

The bright, red ambulance went on its way,
And mom continued to enjoy my wedding day.
But that bright, red color reemerged one December;
This ambulance was for Dad- I'll always remember.
He was taken directly to the ICU,
But there was nothing the doctors could really do.

It was time for him to enter eternal life
Where he could play his silver trumpet with zeal-no strife!
As I entered the chapel near his burial site,
A naval officer played "Taps" so poignantly, so polite.
What happened to me next I'm at a loss to explain;
In fact, some of you might think I'm incurably insane!

When the young officer's "Taps" was reverently completed,
I felt pure love as this tribute was repeated.
So I looked at the soldier with my eyes open wide,
But the shiny, silver trumpet remained still by his side.
I then knew for sure, it was my father, who likewise
Played his shiny, silver trumpet, just for me, from Paradise.

Here I am with my beloved father. We were an awesome team, for sure!

*Here is my handsome dad as a senior and the first chair trumpeter
in the Coventry High School Band in Rhode Island.*

*Here I am, playing a memorial tribute to my dad in
December of 2014, one year after his passing.*

CHAPTER TWENTY-TWO

B ELOW IS A POEM DEDICATED with gratitude to Louise Goffin. I'll always cherish the touching song Louise composed and recorded in memory of my wonderful father. Six months later, her own beloved father, the legendary lyricist, Gerry Goffin, passed away. Gerry wrote such cherished lyrics to many memorable songs. Louise is the producer of the Grammy-nominated CD, *A Holiday Carole*, recorded by her iconic songwriting mother, Carole King. She is also a multi-talented songwriter and musician, who lovingly pays tribute to her dad in her latest EP, *Appleonfire*. Yet, what really matters most is that Louise is a caring, down-to-earth person who has blessed my life in a profound way!

A HEAVENLY VIEW

Remember I am in paradise with no pain or sorrow- a joyful rebirth!
I am truly expressing the depths of my soul in ways that transcend
Even the God-given gifts I was blessed with during my life on this earth.
I will always be your father, your mentor, and your friend.

Your mom's iconic songwriting and my sincere and heartfelt verse
Still give joy to countless fans all over the world and that's quite a rarity,
While touching the lives of generations of devoted, loyal listeners,
The music and the words reflect unique, almost mystical
    complementarities.

I am sending my love down to you and the entire universe.
It's an indescribably beautiful world up here, Louise.

Heaven is ineffably real and so filled with love- no virtual tours.
Life's earthly mysteries are unlocked – I now hold the keys.

I am looking down on you with so much pride and love.
When I see the wonderful woman you are, I truly feel a burst of elation!
Listen closely with your heart, Louise, and I'll whisper my wisdom from
    above.
Language in heaven is simple, yet profound; it needs no translation.

It's very tranquil here up on the roof; It's awesome- this heavenly
    seclusion.
Yet I'm closer to you now, Louise, than I have ever been before.
So far away from the world's chaos and confusion,
I'll always be there, knocking gently on the door.

That is the door to your heart and soul, Louise, my darling daughter.
My words, my music, and my very soul will live on in you.
Sometimes on earth there's no discernible rule or order.
Yet now I can see the beautiful tapestry of my life and it's really a heavenly
    view!

This adorable photo is courtesy of Louise Goffin. This is Louise as an infant, sitting in the lap of her doting father, Gerry Goffin.

Here I am with Louise Goffin after her performance at the Amazing Things
Performing Arts Center in Framingham, MA. (Photo courtesy of Beth Rosen)
Louise is a kind and generous person, and I am very blessed to know her.

CHAPTER TWENTY-THREE

This is a tribute to one of my favorite radio talk show hosts, Dennis Prager.
I had the privilege of meeting him in Sarasota in the fall of 2014.
It was one of the highlights of my life.

DENNIS, THE MENTOR

Like the Rock of Gibraltar, you are steady and strong
As you clarify truths, discerning right from wrong.
Your broadcasting career on numerous stations
Is more suitably described as a true avocation!
As a devout, committed, and religious Jew
You embrace people ecumenically, too!

You respect others' faiths and delightfully converse.
You listen politely and never try to coerce!
You're direct and assertive without ever being rude.
Your passion for truth with an even-tempered mood
Is a refreshing balance in this world of disparity.
You simplify the complicated and focus with clarity.

Your truth-seeking strategies give everyone who listens
A bright glimmer of hope that shines and glistens!
In the midst of the media's histrionics and lies
You sensibly articulate and soundly analyze
Based on both the natural laws and Divine-
The ones that today's world tries to redefine!

Without truth and justice our world falls apart;
Yet, we also need mercy and love in our hearts.
The complementarity of the male and female role
Is truly what makes the family and society whole.
Your exposition of how the "-isms" are so contrived and conflated
Helps us to rediscover the true beauty of the world God created.

The essence of your Ultimate Issues and Happiness Hours
Helps your audience to summon its rational and emotional powers
And harness them to Godly principles and consequently discern
How to properly follow His will, and in turn,
Seek meaning and fulfillment in this hedonistic world.
As we journey toward eternity with our flag unfurled.

You often remind us of our Founding Fathers' intention-
Those moral principles we're often afraid to even mention!
If we could learn the importance of a virtuous life
And appreciate our Founders' sacrifice and strife,
Then, America would truly reemerge as the world's best hope;
But, we must fall on our knees and ask God to help us cope.

So, I thank God for you, my mentor, Dennis.
Yes, there may be some who think you're a menace!
Still, we can only hope and resolutely pray
That the truth, love, and mercy of God will someday
Overcome our divisions and strongly unite
All of us together in His peace, love, and light.

We must all use our talents and gifts, like you,
To enlighten each other with truth and love, too!
While reclaiming the motto, "In God We Trust,"
Putting our words into practice is a must!
So, Dennis, I pray that you'll never cease
To spread God's wisdom, love, joy, and peace!

PART III
Sensory Perceptions

CHAPTER TWENTY-FOUR

RADIATING RHYTHMS: A CIRCLE OF INFINITE JOY AND ELATION!

Dancers freely leaping through space
While spinning at a frenetic pace.
Steady drum beats relentlessly pulsating,
In a whirlwind of motion with tempos undulating.

The momentum builds with increasing velocity,
Spontaneous expressions with unique reciprocity.
There's a deepening awareness of jubilation
That unifies and radiates to the circling congregation.

These feelings transcend what mere words can express;
It's really impossible to ever suppress.
You'll feel a sense of exhilaration!
You're rejuvenated now; it's true liberation!

I love to play drums anytime and anywhere! Playing in a drum circle at nearby beaches is one of my favorite things to do! This is a snare drum made by my paternal great-grandfather, Walter Beauchemin, over 100 years ago.

Yes, I even played with the fabulous Nancy Paolino and the Black Tie Band on my wedding day. What a thrill! Everyone was doing the conga line throughout the venue!

CHAPTER TWENTY-FIVE

Sailing the Ocean Blue- A Natural Refuge

BLUE IS SUCH A LOVELY, SOOTHING COLOR. I'm surrounded by a gorgeous ocean, an endless sea with gentle waves and playful splashes. As I sail along on the serene waters, I gaze up to the royal blue sky, thanking God for my feelings of tranquility.

There's just something about being totally surrounded by the ocean that is so therapeutic. It's like the ocean's tide is just sweeping away all of my worries, woes, and cares. Whatever was gnawing at me before I arrived here has simply evaporated into the air! What seemed so crucial to me upon awakening this morning no longer even registers anywhere within my memory bank. I fondly recall that blue was always my mother's favorite color. I think of her kind, loving ways and feel embraced by her love.

Nature has its own indescribable way of healing in every way- spiritually, physically, and emotionally- if we only allow ourselves to become immersed in its beauty. The ocean is an endless refuge of sparkling, shimmering loveliness.

POETRY IN PERPETUAL MOTION: THE EVER-CHANGING TIDE

The ocean's surface sparkles like jewels.
Yet, hiding beneath its shimmering pools
In the depths of the endless sea,
One discovers such variety!
Stunning sea creatures and effervescent plants

Entice new explorers, spellbound in a trance!
The moving tide propels with energy,
Moving my soul and inspiring me.
Ironically, it seems that my arrival on land,
Is the point when I start to truly understand
The tidal wave of my ruminations,
Which I contemplate with such sweet elation!

CHAPTER TWENTY-SIX

SPRING—AN ANNUAL REBIRTH AND REUNION

The annual reunion is approaching fast.
It's a time to reminisce and renew.
Updating each other and recalling the past,
Shedding a heartfelt tear or two.

The aunts and uncles, siblings and cousins,
All rejuvenated with the aura of spring;
Sometimes telling tall tales by the dozens
As we heartily laugh, embrace, and sing.

Yet there's always a tinge of sorrow,
Remembering our loved ones' passing.
But we know there's a brighter tomorrow,
When we'll join them in life everlasting.

THE KEYS TO SUCCESS

What's still useful and what's obsolete?
Will I continue to save this or just delete?
And to myself I may frequently mutter:
"Someday I'll conquer this clinging clutter!"
So recently a stage of utter antipathy

Transformed into a giant epiphany!
There was really no visible display of a mess;
Still, it was hiding, I must truly confess.
Random items tucked into a variety of spaces,
Occupying numerous and obscure places.
As I sort through these piles of pure miscellaneous,
I separate what's relevant from what's extraneous.
It's a tedious task of clarification,
But a purposeful act of emancipation!
It's incremental change in a chain reaction
While steady progress brings true satisfaction!
As I journey through life I now realize
The need to review and re-prioritize.
It's always a work in progress, I guess;
But clarity and order are the keys to success!

CHAPTER TWENTY-SEVEN

THINGS AREN'T ALWAYS AS THEY REALLY SEEM

Michael Jackson seemed to have it all,
But he succumbed to a drug called propofol.
Elvis Presley was revered as the Rock 'n Roll King,
But his addictions robbed him of his gift to sing.
Karen Carpenter sang these lyrics on occasion:
I'm on the Top of the World, Looking Down on Creation.

Whitney Houston, who once sang so vibrant and strong,
Was overwhelmed by burdens that silenced her song.
I recall Anissa Jones, portraying Buffy, without a care,
On that heartwarming television show, Family Affair.
Yet, sadly she overdosed at age eighteen;
Yes, things aren't always as they really seem.

Perhaps, it's a rainbow today and tomorrow more strife,
It's challenging to maintain a balanced life.
If we choose to focus solely on alluring fame,
We're engaging in a worthless fantasy game.
Someday fame and fortune may fade;
We're left empty inside and completely dismayed.

Celebrities line the red carpet, looking so hip.
They'll proudly promenade, but soon they may trip.

We may witness an enviable public impression,
While the star is enduring a terminal depression.
When our world is artificially contrived,
Are we really in control? Are we really alive?

The applause, the money, and the adulation
Will only cause great consternation
If all we seek are fame, wealth, and power
Or being the prestigious Person of the Hour.
What transcends our earthly existence in time
Is a belief in Divinity, a trust in the sublime.

When I contemplate such talent that was cut short too soon
I'm sure there's some performance behind that big, bright moon!
There has to be a place where all the sorrow, stress, and pain
Transform into a tranquil world that ever more remains.
As I observe the graceful flight of a gentle, peaceful dove,
My hopes likewise take flight to the heavens high above.

My faith reassures me there's Someone beyond
With Whom I share a very close bond.
My earthly journey's often inexplicable,
But my bond with God is inextricable.
The ups and downs of our earthly history,
From rainbows to volcanoes may now seem a mystery.

Life's events are interpreted as the media deems,
But remember things aren't always as they really seem.
If we cooperate with God's plan for us, hence,
I believe life's enigmas will someday make sense.
With God's mercy, we'll experience eternal life
Where there's unspeakable joy and no more strife.

CHAPTER TWENTY-EIGHT

This is a purely fictional account, which simply reflects my thoughts about factors that may impact our interpersonal relationships.

A SIMPLE, CIRCULAR TABLE

I carefully observed the furniture array
That spoke volumes to me that fateful day.
Gone were the desks in rows so tidy,
But still those memories petrified me.
I first came here at the age of twenty;
Decades now passed and the changes were plenty.

I remember that podium so very well
Where our stern professor often gave us hell!
His enormous desk was covered with books,
That he pompously referenced with haughty looks.
These past four decades how much change did ensue!
Not just infrastructure, but the ambience, too.

The desks and chairs so uniform and stable
Had now been replaced by a circular table.
This new arrangement had me quite perplexed.
The circle of my life entered a new context.
Gone were the hideous blackboards and chalk.
We could interact electronically and actually talk.

We engaged in dialogue with no hesitation.
Dr. Jones encouraged our participation!
We congregated around our respected mentor,
With a smiling Dr. Jones drawing us in from the center.
Yes, technology's transformed our lives in a miraculous way,
But my faith in humanity changed at a simple, circular table that day!

CHAPTER TWENTY-NINE

This is another fictional account with reflections on how the pursuit of excessive materialism can negatively impact interpersonal relationships. In this poem, fortunately, a gradual transformation in attitude occurs.

FROM HOLLYWOOD TO CLYDE'S CAFE

At a neighborhood dance
Terry soon caught a glance
Of the tall, slender Kate
Whom he soon wanted to date.
Kate was equally engrossed,
Sharing her Facebook post.

They soon fell madly in love.
It was a true blessing from above.
They only had dated for a mere six weeks,
But their love was the epitome of what we all seek.
Terry had an entrepreneurial mind.
All types of talent he'd attract and find.

He had a penchant for public relations
And was witty and charming on all occasions.
Kate and Terry loved living in LA;
They were enthralled by films, shows, and plays.
Kate had coaxed Terry into a career in PR
And he grew successful in promoting new stars.

Yes, with such stars they had both rubbed shoulders;
But, one day Terry sat with Kate and just told her.
In the celebrity world there are many temptations:
Drugs, alcohol, infidelity, and frustrations.
You see, all that glitters is surely not gold,
Despite the allure that our wealth does hold.

Though fame and fortune ignite many desires,
Where there's a flame, there is certainly a burning fire!
One night as Terry drove his red Lamborghini
To an Italian restaurant for his favorite fettuccine,
It all just hit him like a ton of bricks.
He felt discouraged, disheartened, and so sick.

Kate was waiting for him at their reserved table.
She could tell by his expression that his mood was unstable.
Kate was anxious to learn what that was all about
So Terry just finally blurted it out:
"Hob-knobbing with famous celebrities
Is surely not what it's cracked up to be.

All this status and fortune and wealth
Are simply destroying my formerly good health.
Kate, I love you, but I hardly get to see you."
"Terry, I hear you, and I miss you, too!
I don't want our marriage to be history."
"Kate, solving this dilemma is no mystery.

Yet, if I leave this job, my prestige disappears.
I've built up such clientele these past three years."
"But Terry, I don't care if you work at Lowe's.
You know I love you from your head to your toes.
A prestigious position provides monetary power,
But what's the benefit if our love goes sour?"

"The money's been great, but my job's kept us apart.
I just wish we had this foresight from the start."
So Terry and Kate both vehemently agreed.
Then Terry courageously took the lead,
Applying at Clyde's Cafe to become a barista.
And soon he was promoted to manager.

Eventually they had three boys and a girl.
A true, loving family had now unfurled.
Terry and Kate realized what matters.
They felt blessed to hear the soft pitter-patter
Of their offspring's footsteps and a house full of toys.
The children just multiplied their love and their joy!

They left behind the monetary power,
Resulting in worldly status by the hour.
But Kate and Terry chose a priceless fate.
Terry lost his status, but grew closer to Kate.
They love each other, every day a bit more.
And now it's their children that they truly live for.

CHAPTER THIRTY

This poem is dedicated to my brother-in-law, Dennis Vale. Dennis is an astute observer and commentator regarding current events and the media.

THE SOUND BITE MERRY-GO-ROUND

On the sound bite merry-go-round
We may hear something mundane or profound
An oversimplification of information,
That often reinforces our sense of exasperation.

We hear someone briefly express
Or pontificate more or less
Some useless pabulum- please no more!
Such foolish chatter shakes us to the core!

In turn, we suddenly lose our ability
To patiently rely on logic or civility.
We respond to what's heard by stamping our feet
Or accuse the speaker of being either dumb or elite.

It's easier to simply categorize or label
The person whose opinion seems somewhat unstable.
Like a poisonous mixture in a deadly potion
We erupt with histrionics and unbridled emotion.

Does our media's sound bite proliferation
Negatively impact our powers of concentration?
Can we no longer integrate mind, heart, and soul
Into a healthy and productive whole?

Certainly expressing a point of view
Should never be threatening to me or you.
Yet, it seems in our current society
We've surely lost our sense of propriety.

Granted, we can enjoy the humor in a favorite commercial.
It's good-natured fun- not offensive or controversial.
We can be loyal to our favorite football team
Or gleefully taste our favorite ice cream.

Yet, it seems the prevailing ideology
Shifts our focus from virtue to psychology
Misconduct is inappropriate – not plain wrong!
That's the current mantra- the same old song.

We often hear the pundits say
In our multicultural world today
That life is always changing and all is relative.
Yes, that mode of thought's a tempting sedative.

Suddenly we're not accountable.
Our problems are insurmountable.
Still, can we simply choose to refute
The existence of any moral absolute?

A scintillating sound bite is often reported
And frequently the truth is deeply distorted
The sound bite merry-go-round quickens its pace,
But we keep ending up in the same exact place.

As our cultural norms become ever more permissive,
It's easier to retreat from it all and just be dismissive.
But in a desperate world that needs both truth and love
We must listen with our hearts to the Good Lord above.

Envisioning a Brighter Tomorrow

W ITH EACH DAY COMES A NEW OPPORTUNITY. We can choose to follow a path of righteousness and lead others as well. Or we can take the path of least resistance and wander along with no clear destination.

Today's world needs strong leaders with moral convictions. Strength isn't always displayed with spectacular sights and sounds. It is often experienced with just a whisper, a whisper of spiritual inspiration that touches our soul and moves us to touch the souls of others.

Every Monday afternoon I spend an hour in Eucharistic Adoration in front of the Blessed Sacrament in my parish chapel at the Church of the Incarnation. The atmosphere is completely silent; yet, it is filled with awe. I gratefully join other adorers in worshiping the Lord in the Holy Eucharist and praying for love and peace to spread to all peoples throughout our world. It is truly a heavenly experience to be in the Real Presence of Our Lord.

Often, I just sit there, waiting for the Creator to reveal to me what I am supposed to do next. Sometimes the path I should follow is unclear to me, and I lose my way. Yet, God's infinite mercy always embraces me with forgiveness and reconciliation. Likewise, we must try to unconditionally love and forgive each other.

At the time of this writing, I am looking forward to a very meaningful pilgrimage I will be making with my husband. In October of 2015, fifty-eight years after my parents visited the St. Anne de Beaupre Shrine in Canada, Mike and I will visit there. My parents, who were married later in life, visited the shrine with the express purpose of petitioning for a child. There's no doubt in my mind that St. Anne, the grandmother of Jesus and mother of the Virgin Mary, interceded in a miraculous way.

My mother was told countless times during her pregnancy with me that she would have a miscarriage and simply could not carry a baby to full term. Yet, I was born healthy and strong and essentially remain so currently, despite minor complications from Waldenstrom's. At my birth, my mother was not expected to live, but she made it to almost ninety-four years of age. That was another bonus! So, with Mike by my side, I will thank St. Anne for her intercession to God, who gave me wonderful parents, the gift of an amazing life, and a terrific, loving husband.

Writing my first book has required me to take a step in faith, trusting that God will use my humble efforts in accordance with His unique plan. I hope with each new day, I can pass on to others the love and joy I've experienced at various stages in my life. Thank you for taking the time to read this and may God richly bless you.

Made in the USA
Middletown, DE
03 November 2015